T0347195

not a guide to
Kingston
upon Thames

Simon Webb

First published 2012

The History Press
The Mill, Brimscombe Port
Stroud, Gloucestershire, GL5 2QG
www.thehistorypress.co.uk

British Library Cataloguing in Publication Data.
A catalogue record for this book is available from the British Library.

ISBN 978 0 7524 7968 2

Typesetting and origination by The History Press
Printed in Great Britain

3

Contents

Beginnings: A Royal Borough

There is evidence that the town of Kingston upon Thames was occupied in Roman times and even earlier, during the Stone Age. The first written reference though is in a document from 835, where it is called 'Cyningestun', meaning king's estate or farmstead. A neat piece of folk etymology suggests that the town gained its name from its famous Coronation Stone, but this is not so. A century after the first mention of the town in documents, we read of the 'Royal town which is called Kingston, where coronations are accustomed to be held'. In 1927 the Mayor of Kingston upon Thames petitioned King George V for the right to use the title 'Royal' in the town's name. The king replied, saying that of course this would be fine as Kingston had been described as 'Royal' since 'time immemorial'.

Until 1965 Kingston upon Thames was a town in Surrey. In that year, the increasing sprawl of suburban London was officially recognised and it became the main town of a new outer London borough to be called after Kingston. The title of 'Royal' was transferred to the new borough, which became the Royal Borough of Kingston upon Thames. There are only three other royal boroughs in England; Windsor and Maidenhead, Kensington and Chelsea and, from 2012, Greenwich. The new borough included a number of other villages and towns such as Surbiton and Chessington.

Some Street Names and Their Derivations

Clarence Road

The future King William IV was known before he ascended the throne as the Duke of Clarence. His German-born wife Adelaide was the Duchess of Clarence. When she opened the new Kingston Bridge across the Thames in 1828, the road leading to it was named Clarence Road in her honour. It is now the main shopping street in Kingston.

Clattern Bridge

The oldest street name in the town of Kingston is without doubt that of Clattern Bridge. The earliest reference to the bridge is 'claterynbrugge', probably an onomatopoeic name connected with the clattering of horses' hoofs as they crossed the bridge to the nearby market. The bridge crosses Hogsmill River near to the point where it enters the Thames and is now a Grade I Scheduled Ancient Monument.

Queen's Promenade

Queen Victoria frequently passed through Kingston on the way to Claremont House in Esher, and it is after her that Queen's Promenade is named.

Market Place

The triangular Market Place is laid out just as it was when the market began in Kingston upon Thames in 1170. A market is still held here on six days a week.

10

CLATTERN BRIDGE

Clattern Bridge, which crosses the Hogsmill River, is one of the oldest bridges in Surrey and is a Scheduled Ancient Monument. The earliest known reference is in a deed of 1293 and the medieval name, "Clateryngbrugge", is thought to have been descriptive of the sound of horses crossing the bridge.

The stone arches on the downstream side are the oldest parts of the bridge which until the mid nineteenth century was only 8 feet wide.

ROYAL BOROUGH

OF

KINGSTON UPON

THAMES

Two Kings

Near the Guildhall in the heart of the town of Kingston stands an irregular block of sandstone which was, according to tradition, used for the coronation of seven Saxon kings. It has in the past been supposed that this stone gave its name to the town itself, King's Stone being abbreviated over time to Kingston. For some years, the Coronation Stone stood in the Market Place, where it was used as a mounting block by riders. In 1850, it was set in a special base and surrounded by railings. The names of the Saxon kings who had been crowned near this stone were inscribed around it.

The seven Saxon kings whose coronations were supposedly held at Kingston upon Thames are: Edward the Elder; Athelstan; Edmund I; Eadred; Eadwig; Edward the Martyr; and Ethelred the Unready. It has to be said that there is strong evidence for only two of these actually having been crowned in the town, namely Athelstan and Ethelred.

Athelstan the Glorious (893-939)
Generally regarded as the first king of England and also the first to unite England, Scotland and Wales under one rule, Athelstone was crowned at Kingston in 925. It is a curious circumstance that the first king of the newly unified kingdom should have had his coronation here, rather than in London. The explanation is simple: Kingston stood on the border of the two kingdoms of Wessex and Mercia, while London was for a time in that part of the country known as the Danelaw. In this sense, Kingston was really the heart of England.

Ethelred the Unready (968-1016)
Despite his popular name, Ethelred was not unready in the sense that he was so disorganised that he could never find his crown or get out of bed on time. 'Unready' is a slipshod translation of the Anglo-Saxon word *unread*, which means poorly advised or counselled rather than unprepared.

24-Hour Timeline

00.08 – The first No. 65 bus of the day leaves Kingston, heading for Ealing

00.40 – The first train of the day leaves Surbiton for Waterloo

06.30 – The leisure centre in the Rotunda opens

08.00 – The 'Monday Morning Market' is held at the cattle market

08.30 – Market traders set up their stalls in the Market Place

09.00 – Most shops open

10.00 – Chessington World of Adventures opens its gates

10.30 – Thursday service starts at All Saints' church

11.00 – The Druids Head in the Market Place opens

17.00 – Kingston Tourist Information Centre closes

18.00 – The Bentall Centre closes

23.00 – David Lloyd Leisure Centre closes

23.46 – The last train of the day leaves Kingston for Waterloo

Facts and Figures

The Royal Borough of Kingston upon Thames is on the south-west edge of London. It is bounded on one side by the river Thames and on the others by the county of Surrey and the London boroughs of Richmond, Merton and Sutton and Wandsworth. It is the seventh smallest London borough, with an area of less than forty square kilometres. According to the 2001 census, the borough has the lowest population of any in London with the exception of the City of London. Current estimates vary, but there are probably about 165,000 residents.

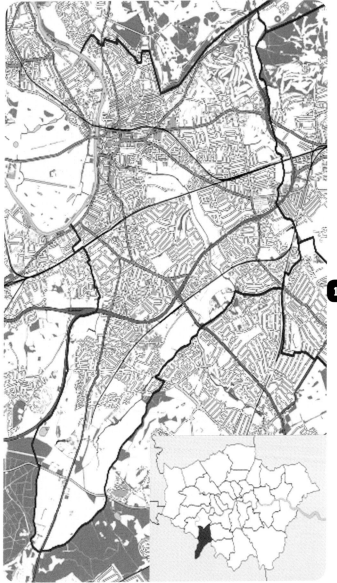

Like most London boroughs, Kingston has seen a steep increase in the number of ethnic minority residents over the last decade or so, from 16 per cent in 2001 to 23 per cent today. The two largest minorities are, rather surprisingly, Koreans and Tamils. The presence of these particular groups is masked in official statistics by being lumped in all together as 'Other Asian'. The town of New Maldon is estimated to have the largest Korean community in Europe. It is thought that the fact that the South Korean ambassador once lived in this area may have something to do with the size of this community.

The Royal Borough of Kingston is a pretty prosperous place. It is, after the City of London and Richmond, the least deprived of the London boroughs. Some indication of how well the district is doing financially may be gauged by the fact that while the average house price in the UK was £161,823 in May 2011, in Kingston it was £305,615. In the United Kingdom as a whole, just over 20 per cent of children are reckoned to live in poverty. In the Royal Borough of Kingston upon Thames, the figure is 15.7 per cent.

The Original Home of Football?

Kingston has as good a claim as any to be the place where the game of football started. This hinges around an exceedingly ancient Shrove Tuesday tradition in the town: two bodies of men fighting for possession of an inflated pig's bladder.

Kingston's game was played on a 'pitch' which extended from Clattern Bridge to Kingston Bridge via the Market Place and Thames Street. Two groups of men essentially re-enacted a famous battle of the eighth century, when the men of Kingston repulsed a group of Viking marauders. The pig's bladder, and later the ball, represented the head of the Vikings' chief.

There were no real rules to the game and over the years many injuries were reported, and quite a bit of damage to shops and other buildings. By the nineteenth century, Kingston was becoming a little more genteel and it was felt that this brutal medieval custom might more comfortably take place in a field rather than through the streets of the town itself. A motion put to the town council on 29 February 1840 claimed that:

> The Game of Football as practiced in this town on Shrove Tuesday is an Obstruction to the passengers, a great annoyance to the peaceable Inhabitants, subversive of good order and prejudicial to the morality of the town.

This attempt to stop the annual game failed and it was not until 1867 that the Shrove Tuesday ritual through the streets was ended for good. These days, the only place in Kingston where you are likely to see a game of football is the Kingsmeadow Stadium in Kingston Road.

Historical Timeline

A number of Roman villas were scattered across the district

Kingston mentioned in the *Domesday Book* as Chingestone

Neolithic farmers tilled the land along the Thames and Hogsmill

First recorded mention of Kingston, when King Egbert calls a Church council

3000 BC **200** **838** **1086**

2000 BC **350** **925** **1264**

Votive offerings were being made at a possible temple site near Eden Street

Athelstan, first king of all England, was crowned at Kingston

Kingston upon Thames was a major centre for the metal trade. Copper was brought by ship from Europe and landed at wharves on the Thames. The smelting of bronze was a major industry in the area.

The town is sacked and burned during the Wars of the Roses

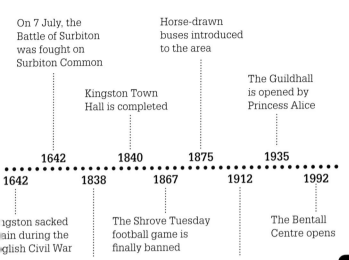

On 7 July, the Battle of Surbiton was fought on Surbiton Common

Horse-drawn buses introduced to the area

Kingston Town Hall is completed

The Guildhall is opened by Princess Alice

1642   **1840**   **1875**   **1935**

1642   **1838**   **1867**   **1912**   **1992**

...ngston sacked ...ain during the ...glish Civil War

The Shrove Tuesday football game is finally banned

The Bentall Centre opens

The first railway line in the district and a station opens in Surbiton

Aircraft manufacture begins in Kingston

Industry

Kingston upon Thames was an important place during Britain's first Industrial Revolution. Metal working began in this country with the manufacture of bronze alloys. Bronze, the first widely-used metal, is an alloy of copper and tin. There is no shortage of tin deposits in Britain, but copper is a little rarer. It was imported by boat from Continental Europe, being landed at wharves in Kingston upon Thames. The tin was carried overland from Cornish mines. At Kingston, the two metals were melted and mixed together to make bronze. At a time when London was a desolate and deserted marsh, Kingston upon Thames was the powerhouse of early British industry.

The *Domesday Book* lists five watermills in Kingston. Later, during the medieval period, the town became famous for brewing. In the nineteenth century, brewing declined and brick-making became more important. It was in 1912 that the industry for which Kingston upon Thames would be known in the twentieth century came to the town. In that year, the manufacture of aircraft began in the town with the founding by Thomas Octave Murdoch Sopwith of the company which would produce over 16,000 military aircraft during the First World War, which began a couple of years later. By 1935, the Hawker Siddeley aircraft factory had become a major employer in the town.

Kingston's association with military aviation continued in the Second World War with the production by the Hawker Siddeley company of the Hurricane fighter. Along with the Spitfire, this airplane came to symbolise the RAF; its appearance being familiar to everybody in the country following the Battle of Britain in 1940. The Hawker Siddley factory in Kingston produced another instantly recognisable plane in 1968, with the Harrier. In 1977, the company was nationalised, becoming British Aerospace. The factory eventually closed in 1992.

Some Famous Buildings and Other Structures

Kingston Bridge

The town of Kingston owes its importance in the past and quite possibly its very existence to the bridge which has crossed the Thames here since at least the thirteenth century. This bridge was of strategic significance militarily, being until the eighteenth century the first bridge upstream from central London. On at least two occasions in British history, Kingston's bridge has played a pivotal role. During the Wars of the Roses in the thirteenth century, an army intent on attacking London was repelled by its citizens. The soldiers hurried to Kingston to cross the river and try an attack from the other side, but were deterred by the men of Kingston.

In 1554, Kingston played an even greater role in the nation's affairs. A rebellion against Queen Mary I led by a Kent landowner called Sir Thomas Wyatt resulted in an army trying to enter London from the South Bank via London Bridge. It was too well defended and so they raced to Kingston, hoping to cross the Thames there and assault London from the north. The citizens of Kingston removed parts of the bridge to impede the rebels' crossing. The delay thus gained gave London time to prepare defences, and Wyatt was defeated.

The Druids Head

The Druids Head in the Market Place is the oldest public house in Kingston. It is a Grade II listed building, dating from the seventeenth century. According to legend, Jerome K. Jerome wrote his famous story of a boat trip along the Thames, *Three Men in a Boat*, while staying at the Druids Head. There is nothing inherently implausible in the idea, as Jerome was very familiar with the town.

Picton House

In 1761, an army officer returning from Africa presented as souvenirs to Sir John Philips, who was living at the time near Kingston: a parakeet, a foreign duck and a five-year-old black slave who was later named Cesar Picton. The position of slaves in Britain was at that time uncertain, and after the deaths of Sir John and his wife, Picton was freed and set up business at Kingston as a coal merchant. He proved to have a flair for business, first renting and then, in 1795, buying outright his premises at No. 52 High Street. So successful was he that he retired and lived the life of a gentleman until his death in 1836 at the age of eighty-one. His business premises and home are still standing and are today marked by a blue plaque. The house is of an unusual design, reminiscent of the American Colonial style.

Surbiton Railway Station

In the 1830s the London and Southampton Railway wanted to build a station at Kingston, but permission to build was refused. The result was that the station was built a mile and a half south of Kingston, at Surbiton. The station opened in 1838, and was rebuilt in 1937 in a brutal, art deco style. It is constructed entirely of white concrete, with a fanciful clock tower to one side. At night, the windows are illuminated from within, giving this suburban station something of the appearance of a small cathedral.

Market House

In the middle of Market Place stands Market House, Kingston's old town hall. It was completed in 1840 and has a vaguely Italian appearance. Its role as town hall ended on the opening of the Guildhall in 1935 and today it houses the Tourist Information Centre.

The Lost Castle

Medieval castles are scattered liberally across the length and breadth of Britain. Most of them are well known: the Tower of London, Caerphilly, Lincoln, Dover and Harlech, to name but a few. Even when they are no longer standing, their ruins are often notable landmarks. It seems impossible to imagine that a stone castle could simply vanish so completely that even its very location has been forgotten. Even stranger to think that such a thing could happen in a built-up part of a London borough!

During the bitter civil wars which rent thirteenth-century England, King Henry III took military action against some rebellious barons. In 1264 he marched to Kingston and besieged the castle belonging to Gilbert de Clare of Gloucester. Rather confusingly, and for reasons which we shall never know, this fortress was known as Warwick Castle. Henry took the castle and there are further mentions of it in the following century. The age of the wooden walled motte and bailey was long over by this time and so it is most likely that this would have been a stout, masonry-built structure in the Norman style.

There is no record at all of Kingston's castle from the fourteenth century onwards and nobody seems to know what became of it. Today, we have not the least idea where it may have stood. The only tantalising clue is that there is a Castle Street in the town. Beyond that, we know nothing at all about this mysterious castle.

Kingston as a Coaching Town

Something which strikes railway travellers as odd is that although Surbiton is on the main line from London to the South Coast, Kingston itself is on a branch line. Since Kingston is by far the biggest town in the area and has always been so, this seems to be a bit of an anomaly. Trains to London are frequent and fast from Surbiton, those from Kingston neither so swift nor regular. The reason lies back in the nineteenth century, when the railways first came to this part of Britain.

Kingston upon Thames lay on the main road between London and Portsmouth. Since this was a major port and where the fleet lay at anchor, it was important that road travel between the two places was as swift and convenient as possible. Kingston became a key town for coaches to change horses and for passengers to be accommodated overnight. As a result of this, very strong commercial interests grew up in the town, which were determined to do nothing to jeopardise Kingston's link with the coaching trade. When in the 1830s a proposal was made by one of the newly formed railway companies to build a line from London to the south of England, passing through Kingston, there was immediate opposition in the town. The entire place was geared to meeting the needs of the coaches and their passengers and permission to build a railway station was refused. The line bypassed the town and a station was built instead at the then hamlet of Surbiton. This station was called Kingston upon Railway.

It was to be another thirty years or so before Kingston had its own railway station, by which time stagecoaches were a ludicrous anachronism. This is why, even though Surbiton is actually slightly further from London than Kingston, getting to London by rail from Surbiton is faster than from Kingston. There are still many traces of Kingston's past as a coaching town. A walk around the area will reveal many old inns with archways by the side to allow coaches and horses to enter.

Bentalls – a Kingston Institution

In 1867, an enterprising young man opened a small draper's shop in Kingston upon Thames. One of his reasons for doing so was to impress his prospective father-in-law by demonstrating his business acumen. The draper's shop flourished. His son Leonard oversaw the expansion of the shop, and by the end of Edward VII's reign, Bentalls were selling furniture, glassware, toys and stationery in addition to drapery. The business thrived and by 1935 had become the largest department store in the country, outside London itself. In that year, a new building was completed for Bentalls. It was an elaborate pastiche of Christopher Wren's additions to Hampton Court: brick, with architectural details picked out in stone. At about this time, the slogan was coined, 'Why go to the West End when there's Bentalls of Kingston?'

Bentalls expanded into other towns, becoming a very 'county' chain of shops. At various times, branches were to be found in Bracknell, Tunbridge Wells, Ealing and even as far afield as Bristol and Worthing. In 1987, work began on a new shopping centre which would have a revamped Bentalls department store at its heart. The Bentall Centre opened in 1992, in a spectacularly modern building which joined seamlessly onto the old brick façade of the pre-war Bentalls. At the heart of the Bentall Centre is an immense atrium, soaring higher than the nave of Westminster Abbey.

Places of Worship

The Lovekyn Chapel

The oldest building in the town of Kingston is the Lovekyn Chapel. Built in the early fourteenth century, it is the only private Chantry Chapel to have survived the Reformation. In Elizabeth I's reign, it was used as a grammar school, and although no longer consecrated as a place of worship, it is still used for civil weddings.

St Raphael's Church

Perhaps the most visually striking church in Kingston is St Raphael's Catholic church in Portsmouth Street. It is a large Romanesque building and, almost unbelievably for such an imposing place, was formerly a private chapel. Built in 1848 for local landowner Alexander Raphael, it looks as though it would be more at home in an Italian village than a London suburb. In 1895, Princess Helene of Orleans, great granddaughter of the former king of France, married here. The wedding was attended by the Prince of Wales, later to become King Edward VII.

There is a possibly apocryphal story that a fortune teller predicted that Alexander Raphael, who was the MP for nearby Surbiton, would die two months after the chapel was consecrated. It is a matter of record that he delayed the consecration three times and did in fact die within a couple of months of the place finally being consecrated.

The Eden Street Temple

It is quite possible that the first place of worship in Kingston pre-dates the town itself. A small Roman altar came to light in the nineteenth century, supposedly unearthed in Eden Street. Since there is not known to have been a town there during the Roman period, its discovery was puzzling. In 1989, archaeological excavations in Eden Street uncovered the remains of a stream bed. Hundreds of coins were found, along with jewellery and rolled up lead sheets (almost certainly curse tablets). The most likely explanation is that a Romano-Celtic temple stood near Eden Street around AD 350 and travellers threw coins into the nearby stream, much as we today throw coins into a wishing well. This may account for the original name of Eden Street, which was Heathen Street.

All Saints' Church

The construction of the present church of All Saints was begun in 1170, but there has been a chapel or church on this spot since the time of the Saxons. Egbert, king of Wessex, held an important council here in AD 838 and until the early eighteenth century, the remains of the Saxon chapel stood near the entrance to All Saints' from the Market Place. This chapel was known as the Chapel of the Coronations, because this is where the famous Coronation Stone was kept and some Saxon kings crowned.

In 1730, the crumbling walls of the Chapel of Coronations collapsed, killing the church sexton. His daughter, Esther Hammerton, was injured by falling masonry, but she recovered and then inherited her father's old job, becoming perhaps the only female sexton in the country. In order to undertake her work of digging graves, she habitually wore men's clothing, at the time a controversial, and almost shocking, thing to do.

Other Places of Worship

Another old place of worship, and one still very much in use, is the Quaker Meeting House in Eden Street. This is a charming eighteenth-century building. There are various other places of worship in the borough, including synagogues, a mosque and a Sikh temple.

FORTVNA
↺ · E · T · ↻
NVMINI
· BVS ·
AVGVSTO
· RVM ·

The Oldest Road Bridge in Britain

Just before Kingston High Street reaches the Market Place, as it passes the Guildhall, it crosses a small bridge. This bridge, which spans the tiny river Hogsmill, is probably unique in this country. A narrow gateway leads down a short flight of steps to the riverside. Looking back at the bridge reveals something very surprising: the arches supporting the bridge on this side are of medieval stonework. The Clattern Bridge was built in 1293, making it the oldest road bridge still being used by traffic in the whole country. It has been extended, strengthened and rebuilt over the years, but the original 600-year-old arches are still supporting a road which today carries an endless stream of buses, cars and lorries from one end of the town to the other.

Local Characters Past and Present

Nipper (1884-1895)

Without doubt, Kingston upon Thames' most famous resident (and the only one to achieve worldwide celebrity) was Nipper. Nipper was a terrier owned by Mark Barraud. On his death, Barraud's brother Francis took on the dog and they lived together in Kingston. When Nipper died, he was buried on the spot now occupied by a branch of Lloyds Bank. Three years after the dog's death, Francis Barraud painted a picture of Nipper the dog listening to a wax cylinder phonograph. This painting, originally entitled, *His Late Master's Voice*, was used as the trademark for the His Master's Voice, HMV, RCA and JVC.

In March 2010, Nipper achieved immortality of another sort when a small road near his grave was renamed Nipper Alley.

John Galsworthy (1867-1933)

John Galsworthy is famous today primarily as a novelist, although during his lifetime he was better known for his plays. He was born into a wealthy family who owned a large estate in Kingston upon Thames. The site of this estate is now occupied by three schools: Marymount International, Rokeby and Holy Cross. Galsworthy's masterpiece is generally regarded as the trilogy known as the Forsyte Saga. When it was dramatised for television in 1967, it caused a sensation. Churches and pubs were empty on Sunday evenings as for six months the whole country was gripped by the affairs of the fictional Forsytes. In 2007, a new building at Kingston University was named after John Galsworthy.

Eadweard Muybridge (1830-1904)

A pioneer of moving pictures, Muybridge worked in America on photographing moving horses and opened the world's first cinema in Chicago in 1893.

Jacqueline Wilson (1945-)

Jacqueline Wilson, the children's author, was born in Bath although she spent most of her childhood in Kingston upon Thames. She left Coombe Girls School at the age of sixteen to take up a job in Scotland. She later moved back to Kingston and lives today in a large Victorian house. Her books, aimed mainly at girls, have sold over 30 million copies in the UK. The main hall at Kingston University is named after Wilson.

John Everett Millais (1829–1896)

Along with Holman Hunt and Rossetti, Millais was a founder member of the Pre-Raphaelite Brotherhood, a nineteenth-century British school of art. He and Holman Hunt moved to Surbiton for the beautiful scenery, which featured in some of their paintings.

William Holman Hunt (1827-1910)

A British painter and co-founder of the Pre-Raphaelite movement.

Cesar Picton (1755-1836)

A successful black businessman, originally from Senegal in Africa. He traded as a coal merchant in Kingston for many years.

Thomas Hardy (1840-1928)

After his marriage on 17 September 1874, Hardy settled in Surbiton.

Enid Blyton (1897-1968)

From 1920 to 1924, Enid Blyton lived at No. 207 Hook Road, Chessington, while she was teaching at a local school. A blue plaque now marks the house.

Petula Clark (1932-)

Petula Clark lived in Chessington and her first ever public performance was singing in the entrance hall of Bentalls department store in Kingston upon Thames in 1939, at the age of seven. Her fee was a box of toffees and a wristwatch.

Julian Clary (1959-)

Julian Clary was born in Surbiton.

The Borough in Fiction

The two places in the Royal Borough which seem to crop up most frequently in fiction are the towns of Kingston upon Thames and Surbiton. Looking first at Kingston, the best description of the town in a work of fiction is that found in chapter six of *Three Men in a Boat* by Jerome K. Jerome. Although a comic novel, *Three Men in a Boat* is also a straightforward account of places along the Thames in the late 1880s. Here is what Jerome says of Kingston at that time:

> The quaint back-streets of Kingston, where they came down to the water's edge, looked quite picturesque in the flashing sunlight, the glinting river with its drifting barges, the wooded towpath, the trim-kept Villas on the other side... the distant glimpses of the grey old palace of the Tudors...

The town also features briefly in H.G. Wells' *War of the Worlds*, when the Martians are advancing on London from their landing places in Surrey. The British army sets up artillery emplacements on Kingston Hill, which are soon destroyed by the heat rays and chemical weapons of the invaders.

More recently, the Bentall shopping centre provided the setting for an episode of the BBC science-fiction series *Primeval*. Dinosaurs were shown rampaging round the place, devouring the hapless security guards.

Surbiton in Literature and the Arts

The very name 'Surbiton' has today an irredeemably comic ring about it for all but those actually living in the town. A good deal of this due to the television comedy series *The Good Life* which was set in Surbiton, although actually filmed in the north London suburb of Northwood. Even before this though, Surbiton had come to epitomise the blameless and respectable life of suburban commuters. It was not always so. At one time, Surbiton was at the heart of British culture and was on the way to becoming a second Chelsea for British artists and writers.

In 1851 two of the greatest English artists of the nineteenth century both moved to Surbiton. John Everett Millais and William Holman Hunt were founding members of the Pre-Raphaelite Brotherhood and they found in Victorian Surbiton a rural idyll perfectly suited to their passion for art portraying a world before the Industrial Revolution. *Ophelia*, regarded as Millais' finest work, shows a stretch of the bank of the river Hogsmill. Holman Hunt's masterpiece *The Hireling Shepherd* has as its background fields in the same area. Holman Hunt's other exceedingly famous picture *The Light of the World* was also painted in Surbiton. The door at which Jesus is knocking was that of a ruined hut which the artist stumbled across on the bank of the Hogsmill. To get the precise effect he wished for, he painted this door in the moonlight, causing the local constable to mistake him for a ghost.

In 1874 Thomas Hardy moved to Surbiton following his marriage. *Far from the Madding Crowd* was published while he lived in the town. The name of naturalist and author Richard Jeffries is not as well known today as Hardy, but he was tremendously famous during the later years of the Victorian Era. He wrote the first post-apocalyptic novel, *After London*, a story in which England sinks into barbarism after a catastrophe destroys most of the human race.

A Remarkable Staircase

Writing of Kingston in 1888, Jerome K Jerome tells the anecdote in *Three Men in a Boat* of a friend of his being shown some old woodwork in a shop:

72

> … the shopman, thereupon, took him through the shop, and up the staircase of the house. The balusters were a superb piece of workmanship and the wall all the way up was oak-panelled, with carving that would have done credit to a palace.

Over 120 years later and the 'superb piece of workmanship'is still in the same place: the site of the Castle Inn, which was built in 1537. The staircase itself is perhaps a century younger than this, generally accepted as being Jacobean. It is an extraordinary piece of work, with dragons and wild men jostling next to elaborately carved foliage.

When the Castle Inn closed down, it was converted to a department store, which in turn became a bookshop and then a branch of Next. Throughout all the repairs, rebuilding and redevelopment, the massive oak staircase has remained in place for over 300 years. It is to be found at Nos 14-16 Market Place.

Law and Order

There was a time when the punishment of criminals was not kept within the walls of prisons, but was made into a public spectacle. Kingston has a lively history of this sort of thing. Sometimes these exhibitions ended in the death of the victim; on other occasions, nothing worse than a loss of dignity resulted.

Fire...

In 1513, for instance, four Lollards in Kingston were arrested and cross examined about their beliefs. The Lollards were followers of John Wycliffe, the man who first translated the Bible into modern English. They were early Protestants and opposed such things as clerical celibacy and the idea that the wafers used during communion actually become the body of Christ. Three of the men being examined decided to recant, but the fourth, Thomas Denys, remained obdurate. On the morning of 5 March 1513, he was led to the marketplace in Kingston, tied to a stake and burned alive for heresy.

… and Water

Like many towns in the eighteenth century, Kingston had a ducking stool. This was used to punish women who were convicted of being scolds or spreading malicious gossip. The woman was tied to the chair, which was attached to the end of a long beam. She was then lowered into a river or pond a few times. This humiliating ritual was designed to prevent women from getting too great an idea of their importance.

Kingston had a ducking stool for at least several centuries. In the Churchwarden's and Chamberlain's accounts for 1672, we find a bill for making a new ducking stool. It cost £1 3s 4d, about £1.17 in decimal currency. There are also frequent items of money listed over the years for repairing the ducking stool. The last record of its having been used in the town was in 1745. In April that year, the landlord of the Queen's Head, an alehouse in Kingston, became so fed up with his wife's nagging that he took her to the magistrates and made an official complaint against her. After hearing both sides of the case, the Justices decided in favour of the man and sentenced his wife to be ducked in the Thames, just downriver from the Kingston bridge.

A crowd of 3,000 people lined the banks of the river to watch the landlord's wife being strapped into the ducking stool and lowered until she was completely submerged in the water.

A Horrible Death

William Way was born at Exeter in 1560. He was a devout
Roman Catholic at a time when this was a hazardous religion
to follow. As a young man, he travelled to the Continent,
where at the age of twenty-four he was ordained as a priest.
Elizabeth I was on the throne at this time and had declared
herself head of the Church as well as monarch. Failure to
accept her status in the Church was regarded as treason.

In 1586, William Way returned to England and was swiftly
arrested. He spent some time in prison before being brought
to court. His refusal to acknowledge Queen Elizabeth as
head of the Church was enough to seal his fate. The fact that
the Spanish Armada, an invasion fleet intending to restore
Catholicism to England, had recently been defeated by
Francis Drake could not have helped matters.

On 23 September 1588 William Way was brought to the
Market Place in Kingston and underwent one of the most
agonising forms of death ever devised: hanging, drawing
and quartering. He was hanged long enough to suffer the
pains of strangulation and then cut down while alive and
conscious. He was then castrated and his intestines pulled
out and burnt. Finally, his body was dismembered and his
head cut off.

Væ qui dicitis malum bonum, & bonum malum:
ponentes tenebras lucem, & lucem tenebras ponentes amarum in dulce, & dulce in amarum. Esa. 5.

Kingston and Surrounding Towns During the English Civil War

Modern day Kingston upon Thames might be something of a backwater, a quiet little town on the edge of the capital, but on several occasions in the past it was pivotal in the nation's affairs. One such time was the English Civil War, which took place in the seventeenth century. Kingston was sympathetic to the King's cause and had moreover an important military arsenal. Soon after Parliament went to war with the King, a message was sent by the Parliamentary forces to Kingston to see where it stood. The reply was unsatisfactory and so the Roundheads took the town, where they found the population hostile, surly and 'full of malignant humours', to quote a contemporary observer.

Kingston was later occupied by the Royalists and the king himself visited the town. The strategic significance of the place was, of course, the bridge. Anybody wishing to attack London from either the north or south could cross the river at Kingston and approach the capital from whichever direction seemed best. There seem to have been a lot of Royalist sympathisers in the area. At Chessington there was a fortified manor house which was being used as a Royalist base. Cromwell's soldiers assaulted this and burnt it to the ground. This accounts for its local name in later centuries of 'Burnt Stub'. This rebuilt mansion is now Hocus Pocus House in Chessington World of Adventures.

Surely one of the least known and most improbably named incidents in the entire English Civil War took place on 7 July 1648. This was the so-called Battle of Surbiton. A force of about 600 cavalry loyal to the king mustered at Kingston before heading south towards the coast. Charles I was being held on the Isle of Wight and the idea was to take a ship and rescue him. The cavalry got no further than Surbiton Common before being intercepted by a Parliamentary force from Windsor. The skirmish was bloody and decisive, ending in the rout of the Royalists. The Civil War ended a few months later.

Eadweard Muybridge and the World's First Cinema

The late nineteenth century saw the emergence of moving pictures and the birth of the cinema. A crucial figure in this developing technology was born and died in Kingston, although living much of his life in the USA. Edward James Muggeridge was born in 1830 and emigrated to America in 1855, where he changed his name to Eadweard Muybridge. The reason for the eccentric spelling of the first name was that he wished to spell his Christian name in the same way as one of the Saxon kings crowned at Kingston.

Muybridge became a skilled and well-known photographer and it was in this capacity that he became embroiled in the so-called 'Galloping Question'. There was much debate as to whether or not all four of a horse's hooves left the ground simultaneously when it was trotting, cantering and galloping. The legs move so swiftly that it is impossible to resolve this question by visual observation alone. Muybridge hit upon the ingenious idea of arranging twelve cameras at intervals of a foot or eighteen inches, each one triggered by a thread. He then got somebody to trot a horse past them and obtained a sequence of a dozen photographs showing every stage of movement of the horse's legs. One shot showed clearly that all four hooves were off the ground at the same time.

By attaching these pictures to the parlour toy known as the zoopraxiscope, Eadweard Muybridge was able to produce the illusion of movement – the first moving pictures, in fact. At the 1893 World Exposition in Chicago, Muybridge had a special building called the Zoopraxographical Hall in which he showed his moving pictures to the public for a charge. This was the world's first commercial exploitation of moving pictures – the earliest cinema.

The following year, Eadweard Muybridge returned to England. He died in Kingston ten years later at No. 2 Liverpool Road. In 2004 a plaque was unveiled on the side of this house, commemorating Muybridge's work and his role in the creation of the modern cinema.

An attempt was made to recreate Muybridge's work a few years ago but it failed, despite the vast leaps in technology since his time. The reason was an odd one. Muybridge's technique relied upon horses trotting into and breaking thin threads. It proved impossible to find a modern horse that would trot straight into a string or thread, because they are mostly familiar with electric fences from their earliest days. These are just white tapes strung between poles. There is an inherent fear of heading directly at something from which they have in the past received a shock.

Local Wildlife

For a London borough, Kingston has an astonishing variety of wildlife. This is due to the semi-rural nature of the local authority area, which until 1965 was part of Surrey. Everything from foxes and deer to parrots and terrapins are to be found living wild, sometimes even within built-up areas. Herons, for example, have been observed perched on old shopping trolleys in the Hogsmill, right in the centre of Kingston. Even kingfishers have been seen diving into the Hogsmill at Kingston.

Kingston's Parrots

It may surprise readers who do not live in South East England to hear that parrots, specifically ring-necked parakeets, are a common garden bird in the borough. There are several possible explanations for the prevalence of such exotics birds so far from their native haunts in India.

The most likely origin of the parrots, which some now regard as a pest in Surrey, is that they escaped from the old Isleworth film studios, about four miles from Kingston itself. In 1951, scenes from the film *The African Queen* were being shot in a large water tank there. In order to create verisimilitude, a flock of ring-necked parakeets were released in the studio and allowed to flutter around Humphrey Bogart and Katherine Hepburn as they pretended to be struggling through a river in the Congo. The rumour is that by a mishap some of these birds escaped and formed the nucleus of a breeding colony along the Thames.

Whatever the truth of the *African Queen* story, and it may be no more than an urban legend, the fact remains that ring-necked parakeets are now to be found in large numbers throughout the whole borough, where they are one of the commonest birds.

Terrapins in the Hogsmill

Hogsmill River flows through the borough of Kingston upon Thames, entering the river Thames just after passing under Clattern Bridge in the centre of town. A number of terrapins live in the Hogsmill and may sometimes be seen sunning themselves on its banks. Their origin is less mysterious than that of the ring-necked parakeets. Following the success of the television cartoon series *Teenage Mutant Ninja Turtles* in the 1980s, a number of parents bought red-eared sliders, a type of turtle, as pets for their children. Although small and cute to begin with, these terrapins grown after a year or two until they weigh two kilograms and are about fourteen inches long. They are also very aggressive, living in the wild on frogs and water birds.

Once they reached a certain size, many parents surreptitiously released them into the wild, where they adapted with surprising ease to the British climate. They have been known to attack and kill ducks.

'Out of Order'

In December 1989 a dramatic piece of contemporary art was unveiled in Kingston. From the very beginning, it was hugely controversial. Michael Mannal, the then mayor, who gave a speech before the sculpture was revealed, said later that he had to get a council officer to write his speech, because his own views would have been unprintable!

So what was this work of art? It consisted of twelve old red telephone kiosks toppling over like a line of dominoes. The man who created it, David Mach, is no stranger to controversy: he created a full size replica of the Flying Scotsman in Northumberland, built from 185,000 bricks.

Eleven years after 'Out of Order', which was what Mach's telephone boxes were called, was erected, local traders were petitioning to have it removed from Old London Road. It was claimed that this strange piece of work was becoming dilapidated and turning into an eyesore. Twelve years down the line though and 'Out of Order' has become something of a symbol of modern Kingston. Indeed, it features on the borough's Olympic logo. Instantly recognisable, the people of Kingston now seem very fond of their weird work of public art and nobody has a bad word to say about it.

Famous For

Being one of the few royal boroughs

Military aircraft

The dog on HMV records

The nearest theme park to London

Being mentioned in *Three Men in a Boat*

Bentalls

Pretending to be still in Surrey, while remaining a London borough

Jacqueline Wilson

Infamous for

Phyllis Dixey

Phyllis Dixey was born in Merton in 1914. She worked in music halls and entertained troops in ENSA during the early years of the Second World War. In 1942, she put together a troupe of girls and rented the Whitehall Theatre in London, putting on a show called *The Whitehall Follies*. This was the first striptease show ever staged in the capital and earned Phyllis the title of 'Queen of Striptease'. It was all pretty tame by today's standards: one turn involved Phyllis Dixey reciting poetry without any clothes on!

You might think that, by 2011, such capers would be no more than an historical curiosity, and in any other part of the country but Surbiton, you would probably be right. When, however, English Heritage wished to commemorate the life of Britain's first real striptease artiste by putting a blue plaque on the block of flats where she once lived in Surbiton, they soon encountered ferocious opposition to their plans. Residents argued that such a thing would lower the tone of the building. A striptease artiste mentioned on the side of Wentworth Court! Whatever next?

There is something deliciously genteel about this controversy and wholly in keeping with the traditional image of Surbiton which we know and love from *The Good Life* and *Monty Python*. One resident said, with an apparently straight face, 'The word striptease leads you to certain visual images'. All too true. 'I know this is her history, but I would want it to be said in the nicest way possible'. The nicest way possible! In Surbiton, stripping is definitely still regarded as being 'not quite nice'.

Letters to Local Newspapers

There is something oddly reassuring about reading the letters to local papers in areas other than the one you yourself live in. We are used to the astonishingly trivial and parochial concerns of our own neighbourhood and it sometimes crosses our mind that perhaps it is just where we live and that the people who write to their local rag in more exotic or affluent locations might be different from the strange characters who express their concerns to the editor in our neck of the woods. Speaking in general, they are not.

Consider the mind-numbingly pointless letter sent to the *Surrey Comet* by a resident of Waters Road in Kingston on 13 January 2012. The writer was concerned that for the last twenty-one years she had been receiving Christmas cards addressed to a Miss Lesley Hill. She was puzzled, because she had bought the house in 1991 from two people called Mick and Chris; how long ago, she wondered, did Leslie Hill live there? Rest easy: the sort of people who write to the editor of their local paper are a pretty loopy bunch wherever one lives!

Headlines

In November 2008, Chessington Zoo hit the headlines, but not perhaps in the way that they would have chosen. Inspectors from the Department for Environment, Food and Rural Affairs criticised the fencing around the enclosures containing the lions and tigers. Specifically, they were worried that it was not secure enough and that the big cats might be able to get out and eat visitors to the theme park and zoo. Chessington World of Adventure indignantly responded that the safety of their visitors was paramount. That fears about the security of the enclosures were not entirely groundless was demonstrated on 26 May 2011.

It was a glorious day in early summer and Chessington Zoo was thronged with visitors. Visitors to the lion enclosure were surprised to see what appeared to be two animated cuddly toys clamber over fences and enter the enclosure. They were baby binturongs, adorable, cuddly little creatures which look like teddy bears. In an instant, one of the creatures was seized upon by a lion and as horrified families gaped in disbelief was torn to pieces and eaten by the rest of the pride. The other binturong literally died of fright. Whether or not the lions could get out, it was clear that other things could certainly get in, and Chessington Zoo promised an investigation.

Kingston's Market

Trade has taken place in the Market Place at Kingston for almost 800 years. These days, nothing more than fruit and vegetables are sold there, but the history of the market stretches back many centuries. It was originally established in 1242 and flourished for the next 350 years. It was not only people actually living in the town who came to market: it drew farmers and shoppers from all the neighbouring districts as well. In 1603, James I granted a new market at Kingston, which was to be held on Saturdays. This was a livestock market and also a place to buy and sell grain. The town council managed to regulate the price of the grain being sold here and boasted that they had succeeded in driving down the price of a bushel of wheat from 9*s* 6*d* to 7*s*.

By 1619, a fish market had been set up and was very popular. The cattle market at Kingston was still going strong in the nineteenth century, but as the town became more urban, this market gradually faded away. The triangular Market Place is still the centre of the town today and the buildings around it still show the original shape of this part of the town, exactly as it was in the early thirteenth century.

A Famous Man

Most towns have some notable figure who has been very important in the history of that particular location but is wholly unknown in the wider world. Such a man was Henry Shrubsole, three times Mayor of Kingston. Born in 1817, Shrubsole was active in Kingston's civic life, being elected mayor for the first time at the age of sixty in 1877. He was elected mayor again the following year and then once more in 1879. He died in office, dropping dead unexpectedly during a public engagement on 18 January 1880.

In Memory of
William Shrubsole,
who died March 19th 1848,
Aged 73 Years.

And of Elizabeth, his wife,
who died Oct. 26th 1864,
Aged 78 Years.

"In hope of eternal life." Titus 1. 2.

This tablet is erected
by their surviving children
Sarah Rumgard and Mary Booth.

Henry Shrubsole was born into a family of undertakers. This proved such a profitable concern in the late eighteenth and early nineteenth centuries that the business expanded and then branched out into first drapery and then banking. Shrubsole's Bank was a Kingston institution during the heyday of Queen Victoria's reign. Towards the end of the century, though, the smaller, family-run private banks were swallowed up by the bigger companies and Shrubsole's Bank was absorbed by the National Westminster.

Henry Shrubsole has a very impressive monument, which is admired daily by all who pass it. Situated in the Market Place, directly in front of the old Market Hall, it is a water fountain, surmounted by a statue of a woman carrying a water jug and accompanied by a child. At the base is a sculpted likeness of Henry Shrubsole's face in profile. In 1999, this fine piece of work acquired Grade II Listed status.

Jane Austen

Jane Austen, the famous writer, had a soft spot for Kingston upon Thames. Not only was she familiar with the town and enjoyed passing through it, she also used it in both a literal and metaphorical sense in *Emma*.

There were two routes from Jane Austen's home in Surrey to her brother's house in London. One took her through Clapham and Battersea and the other passed through Croydon and Kingston. The road to Kingston was along the Hogsback, an eleven-mile long hill which provided panoramic views over the countryside. Writing to her sister in 1798, Jane says, 'Our route tomorrow is not determined. I think we shall go through Croydon and Kingston, which is much pleasanter than any other way.'

In *Emma*, Mr Knightley goes regularly to Kingston on business. Another character in the book, Mr Martin, also goes there a number of times. This device is used to indicate to the reader that although in Emma's eyes the two men are very different in both character and social standing, they are in many ways essentially similar. Both are decent, good-hearted men who travel to Kingston on business.

EMMA:

A NOVEL.

IN THREE VOLUMES.

———◆———

BY THE

AUTHOR OF "PRIDE AND PREJUDICE,"
&c. &c.

———◆———

VOL. I.

═══════════

LONDON:

PRINTED FOR JOHN MURRAY.

———

1816.

The Swans of Kingston

It is the one thing that everybody knows about swans: they belong to the Queen. Well, almost right. Over the years, British monarchs have lost their taste for roast swan and now claim ownership only of some of the mute swans on the Thames and its tributaries. Even here, the Crown does not exercise exclusive rights. Since the fifteenth century, the monarch has shared the swans with the Vintners' Company and the Dyers' Company, two of the Livery Companies of the City of London.

What is Kingston's connection with all this? The ceremony of Swan Upping, which takes place every summer, is essentially a census of the Thames' swans. Some are nominally claimed by the Queen and others by the two companies. The post of Keeper of the Queen's Swans was for many years held by members of the Turk family of Kingston. The last Turk in this role, John Turk, held the post for thirty years until his death in 1993 at the age of eighty-two. When he died, the position of Keeper of the Queen's Swans was abolished and replaced by two new posts: Warden of the Swans and Marker of the Swans.

The Turk family of Kingston have another longstanding association with the Thames: they are the proprietors of Turk Launches and have been building and operating boats in the town for many years. Some of their boats were bought by Queen Victoria.

Picture Credits

Page: